WINNING WORDS

Susie Dent

OXFORD
UNIVERSITY PRESS

OXFORD
UNIVERSITY PRESS

Great Clarendon Street, Oxford OX2 6DP

Oxford University Press is a department of the University of Oxford.
It furthers the University's objective of excellence in research, scholarship,
and education by publishing worldwide in

Oxford   New York

Auckland   Cape Town   Dar es Salaam   Hong Kong   Karachi
Kuala Lumpur   Madrid   Melbourne   Mexico City   Nairobi
New Delhi   Shanghai   Taipei   Toronto

With offices in

Argentina   Austria   Brazil   Chile   Czech Republic   France   Greece
Guatemala   Hungary   Italy   Japan   Poland   Portugal   Singapore
South Korea   Switzerland   Thailand   Turkey   Ukraine   Vietnam

Oxford is a registered trade mark of Oxford University Press
in the UK and in certain other countries

British Library Cataloguing in Publication Data

Data available

ISBN 978-0-19-919874-0

7   9   10   8

Printed in China by Imago

Acknowledgements

The publisher would like to thank the following for permission to reproduce
photographs: **pp6, 7** Granada TV/Susie Dent, **p17** Corbis/Sunset Boulevard/Kipa, **p18** BBC
Photo Library, **p19** By permission of the Secretary to the Delegates of Oxford University Press

The publisher would also like to thank the following:
Rowan Atkinson for allowing us to use his image on page 18
Philip Cieslik of Yorkshire Television for the use of all Countdown images

Illustrations by David Mostyn

Extract from *Blackadder: The Whole Damn Dynasty* by Richard Curtis and Ben Elton
(Michael Joseph, 1998), copyright © Richard Curtis and Ben Elton 1987, reprinted by permission of PFD
on behalf of Richard Curtis, Berlin Associates on behalf of Ben Elton and Penguin Books Ltd.

Every effort has been made to contact copyright holders of material reproduced in this book.
If notified, the publishers will be pleased to rectify any errors or omissions at the earliest opportunity.

Contents

Why language matters

Language is all around us. We need it for most of the activities in our daily lives and for almost every kind of human communication. We use it when we speak, when we read, when we write, when we text and email – even when we think. Babies begin to understand words in their first year of life.

The language we use is recorded in dictionaries, which help us to understand words and to use them correctly. The way we speak and write is constantly changing, and new dictionaries – whether they are printed or electronic – are always trying to catch up. In fact our language, English, is the fastest-changing language in the world.

Our vocabulary changes when:

- brand new words are invented
- old words take on new meanings.

enagers

n Talki

it How r u? will

Did you know?

Completely new words make up only 1% of all the changes to our language. The simple 'recycling' of old words accounts for over 15% of all the changes. The majority of new words by far, however, are variations of older words made into something new (see pages 12–13 to see how).

We sometimes take language for granted. We don't really, for example, need to think about how we write a shopping list or gossip with our friends. Recently, however, the way we use language has become a hot topic. Today's newspapers have regular features about words in the news, and teenage magazines frequently use and explain the latest **slang**.

On TV too, language is a popular subject. Many quiz shows are based on language games such as crosswords, **anagrams,** or catchphrases. One of the most famous of these is *Countdown*.

Countdown began in 1982 and is one of the longest-running TV quiz shows in the world. Britain's *Channel 4* had just been launched and *Countdown's* host, Richard Whiteley, was the first face to appear on it. The show's simple format has changed very little since then. Richard and his co-presenter, Carol Vorderman, are two of the most familiar faces on British television today.

Countdown is a battle of words and numbers between two contestants. In the word-games, each contestant must come up with the longest word they can from a selection of nine letters. So, for example, from the letters:

S T I L D I V E S

you could find the word 'dives' for five letters (scoring 5 points for a five letter word), 'tidies' for six letters (6 points) or 'visited' for seven letters (7 points), and so on. The *Countdown* team couldn't find a longer word than that from this selection: well done if you can!

Each programme has eleven of these letter-games, three number games, and one *Countdown* conundrum (an anagram of nine letters). At the end of this book you can test yourself on some actual *Countdown* letter games from past shows. Meanwhile you will also find anagrams thoughout this book (see below) for you to unscramble. **Warning: they get harder as you go along!**

Anagram – unscramble these letters to make a word:

T R C A R O

Why does language change?

It is fascinating to think that language never stands still. Will people living in a century's time be able to understand the words we use? We often need help to understand William Shakespeare's language, after all. So why does language keep changing?

The first thing to remember is that language does not move by itself: it changes because we need it to. Every new technological, medical or scientific development, every new type of music or art, needs a name. Some of these areas are moving so fast that language needs to be very quick to keep up. Think of computing and the Internet, for example, or of mobile phone technology. New words in these areas are emerging all the time.

Do you use text messages? If so, are you tempted to use text **abbreviations**, such as '4' for 'for', '2' for 'to' or 'too', and 'r' for 'are', in written notes to your friends, or in emails? If so, you're not alone. Some people even predict that these will become acceptable English within the next few decades.

Other big influences on our language are music and television. Words from rap music such as *bling-bling* (describing showy jewellery or clothing), and *crib* (your home or house), are now used as part of everyday slang. Our favourite TV programmes are another powerful way of spreading new words. The American series *Friends* is said to have made *so* (as in *'That is so not nice'*) a **catchword** for a whole generation. In this case TV was spreading something which already existed in parts of America. It can also be the creator of completely new words or phrases, including catchphrases.

Can you think of some catchphrases from popular TV programmes, or from films? Here are a few to start you off:

Booyakasha!: all right! *(Ali G)*

Five by five: **perfect, cool** (from *Buffy the Vampire Slayer*)

Doh! (Bart Simpson in *The Simpsons*)

The truth is out there (The X-Files)

May the force be with you (Star Wars)

Big Brother is watching you (Big Brother)

Where do new words come from?

You might expect new words to be the colourful inventions of a single person at a single moment in time. In fact, only 1% of all new words come about in this way. Most are the result of other things happening to our language.

Did you know?

It is not just our vocabulary which changes — our grammar and our pronunciation are also constantly shifting. Today it is considered wrong to say 'ain't it?' for 'isn't it?', but a few hundred years ago it was used by the kings and queens of Britain. It was also considered correct to say 'you was' rather than 'you were' in the eighteenth century.

Boring, ain't it? We are not amused!

The old and the new

New words are often old words which have been given new meanings. Almost every word that we use has had a variety of different meanings over time. In many cases, the old meanings will remain, alongside the new ones. Slang offers particularly good examples of this. It is one of the fastest-moving areas of language. Today, 'sick' can mean 'excellent' as well as 'disturbed' or 'ill'.

Mixing and matching

New words are also created when we combine existing words, or parts of them, to create something different. **Prefixes**, such as 'un–', 're –', and 'out' in front of a word, and **suffixes** at the end of words such as '–y' (as in 'dirty'), can be used to create hundreds of new words. Words can also be blended together, either as a whole or in parts. The results are often surprising. Can you guess which words combined to produce the following recent new words? They may not stand the test of time, but they are certainly colourful!

chofa

frienemy   globesity

Why not have a go at inventing some colourful new words yourself using this 'blending' technique? Try it with parts of words: we will look at combining whole words later. You might end up with some fun results!

Anagram – unscramble these letters to make a word:

N I M G R O N

Brand new?

Some of the words we use as part of everyday English were originally **brand names**. If a product is successful enough in its field its name can be used in a general way:

- we use the word 'hoover' for all sorts of vacuum cleaners, not just those made by the *Hoover* company

- we may say we have taken an 'aspirin' when we might have taken a different sort of tablet that doesn't actually contain any aspirin.

Words from afar

Some English words have travelled a long way. Many of the words we use are originally from Latin or Greek. Today, countries and cultures from all corners of the world are influencing our vocabulary.

Can you guess where the following everyday words came from originally?

futon

silhouette

kindergarten

spaghetti

ketchup

Keeping it short

One of the fastest growing areas of language is in the use of **acronyms** and abbreviations. Text messages and emails are introducing hundreds of new abbreviations, such as 'LOL' ('lots of love' or 'laugh out loud') and 'BTW' ('by the way'). Can you think of a few more?

English around the world

Did you know that there are hundreds of varieties of English in addition to British and American English? TV and the Internet are bringing many new 'English' words over to us. Australian English, for example, has a strong influence on British English because of TV soaps such as *Neighbours*. A lot of our new words also come from Indian English, Caribbean English and South African English.

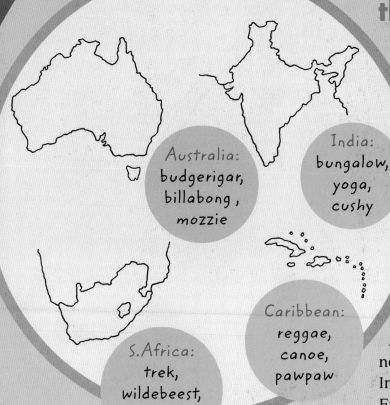

Australia:
budgerigar,
billabong,
mozzie

India:
bungalow,
yoga,
cushy

S.Africa:
trek,
wildebeest,
comandeer

Caribbean:
reggae,
canoe,
pawpaw

The really new

There is a term in the music industry to describe singles which are becoming popular but which haven't quite made it – yet. They are said to be 'bubbling under'. Some words do the same. They begin to be used by more and more people and may last long enough to make it into the language 'charts': a dictionary. As we've seen, some of these words will be 'cover versions' of older ones. Some, however, will be brand new. How do they come about?

A lot of brand new words are from science and technology, where a new invention needs a new name. Others come from the books we read. Did you know that William Shakespeare was one of the greatest inventors of new words? We still use hundreds of words that he invented. 'Lonely', 'excitement', 'fashionable' and 'unreal' were all **coined** by him. Today, authors such as J.K. Rowling, creator of the *Harry Potter* stories, are creating new words for their fictional worlds. Some of them may even make their way into everyday English.

Wizardy Words

Mixing and matching

As well as inventing new words, J.K. Rowling also plays with existing ones. Many of these are **compounds**: combinations of existing words. 'Spellotape', for example, is magical repair tape used by wizards. Try putting together some of the words below to create five new ones of your own. Give each of them a **definition** in the style of a dictionary, e.g. a 'mudmint' could be: a magic sweet which squelches in your mouth and turns your tongue brown.

time   worm

slug   mud

mint   fizz

wand   bomb

mouth   jelly

blood   cauldron

Anagram – unscramble these letters to make a word:

O O M T A T E S

How does a word get into a dictionary?

If you were to invent a new word, how would it get into a dictionary?

Dictionaries are written by **lexicographers**, who look at real language as it is written and spoken today. As a general rule, before a word can get into an *Oxford* dictionary it has to be mentioned:

- five times

- over five years

- by five different sources.

This may sound easy, but these rules are a tough challenge to meet. It isn't enough for a word to be used a lot by a small group of people. It needs to be used by the outside world and to show real staying power.

A new word also needs to be:

- *useful* – a new scientific discovery such as *DNA*, for example, needs a name to describe it

- *easy to remember* – if a word is difficult to pronounce, for example, it can be easily forgotten

- if a word is both of these it is much more likely to be *used*, which is crucial if it's going to survive.

Some of the latest words to have made it into a dictionary are given below. Which of the two requirements (useful/easy to remember) do you think each of them fits?

bioweapon: a harmful biological agent used as a weapon of war

cybercrime: criminal activities carried out by means of computers or the Internet.

show pony: (informal) an attractive, stylish, or flamboyant person, especially a performer, who enjoys being in the limelight

threequel: the third film, book, event, etc., in a series; a second sequel

talkboard: an Internet bulletin board or chat room

va-va-voom: the quality of being exciting, vigorous, or attractive

Did you know?

New languages are being created all the time by particular groups of people. Fans of the TV series *Star Trek* have developed the language 'Klingon', which was spoken in the series by the alien race of warriors. 'Elvish', meanwhile, is a group of languages invented by the writer J.R. Tolkien for such stories as *Lord of the Rings*.

How did dictionaries begin?

The way dictionaries are **compiled** has changed a lot since the first records of language were made almost three hundred years ago. Samuel Johnson's *Dictionary of the English Language*, which was published in 1755, was the first serious attempt to capture English in a dictionary.

The 1980s British comedy series *Blackadder* included a **sketch** of Samuel Johnson presenting his dictionary to the royal court. The following dialogue is a good and funny example of the difficulty of trying to catch language before it changes again. Blackadder's strange words are, of course, made up, but the sketch shows us that no dictionary can ever include every single word that we use. Language simply moves too quickly.

Johnson: This book, sir, contains every word in our beloved language!

Blackadder: Every single one, sir?

Johnson: Every single word, sir!

Blackadder: Oh. Well, in that case, sir, I hope you will not object if I also offer the Doctor my most enthusiastic... contrafibularities.

Johnson: What?!

Blackadder: Contrafibularities, sir? It is a common word, down our way.

. . . .

Blackadder: Leaving already, Doctor? Not staying for your pendigestatory interluditude?

Johnson: No, sir! Show me out!

Blackadder: Certainly, sir! Anything I can do to facilitate your velocitous exteriorilisation.

In 1861, work began on the *Oxford English Dictionary*. Known as the *OED*, it is the largest dictionary of English ever published. Work on this huge project carries on today, with a large team of lexicographers updating definitions of existing words, or drafting definitions of new ones.

This photo shows James Murray, who spent over half a century on completing the first edition of the *OED*. Examples of how words were used were collected on pieces of paper known as 'quotation slips', which were stored in alphabetical 'pigeon holes'. There were no computers in those days to hold all that information!

Anagram – unscramble these letters to make a word:

F U H O E P L

Dictionary-making today

Today's lexicographers have at their fingertips thousands of examples of how we are using language every day. They use databases – huge stores of information held on a computer – containing hundreds of millions of examples of written and spoken language. These come from almost every area you can imagine – from medicine, science, and history, to modern novels, comics, and even Internet chat rooms. A lexicographer can search the databases for examples of the word or phrase for which they need to write the definition.

So how is an **entry** written?

Collecting evidence

The first step in creating or revising an entry is to look at evidence of words and phrases in use from all over the English-speaking world. Imagine it to be like looking through a photo album, except that in this case the photos are snapshots of language and how we are using it. Look at the example below, taken from the *Oxford Dictionary of English*, for the verb 'end'. Each represents one way in which people are currently using the word.

end
Mario led the race from beginning to *end*.
The party called an *end* to violence.
If she so much as makes a sound, that'll be the *end* of her.
'Hello' said a voice at the other *end*.
He reached the *end* of his tether.
You could *end* up with a higher income.

Writing the definition

By looking at how a word is used, lexicographers can pinpoint its meaning. The definition of the word is based on this 'picture' of the language.

Word origins

Some dictionaries will tell you where a word came from and how it came about. The *OED* is a 'historical dictionary', and it gives the various meanings of each word as it has travelled through time. Some of these word histories are very interesting. Most of us know that 'bad' and 'wicked' can now mean 'excellent' in today's slang, but did you know that 'silly' once meant 'deserving sympathy' before it went on to mean 'foolish'? Or that 'nice' meant 'silly' 800 years ago? It has also meant 'strange' and 'lazy' along the way. All of these examples demonstrate how English is forever changing.

How long does it all take?

The amount of time it takes to write a complete dictionary entry can vary widely, but for a typical word, with just one meaning, a complete entry might take a few hours to prepare. A more complex word, such as 'take', which is used in hundreds of ways, may take days to complete.

How dictionaries work, and why we need them

If language is constantly changing, how can dictionaries be useful? The answer is that, even though dictionaries can never be totally up to date, most of the words they include have been around for a very long time. Changes to the meanings of those words can take many years. As a result, dictionaries are still very valuable tools in helping us to understand each other. They give us:

- the meanings of words we encounter for the first time

- correct spellings

- help on choosing the right word for the right situation.

Finding your way

At the top of each dictionary page you will see a *guide* word. On the left-hand page the guide word is the very *first* word. On the right-hand page the guide word is the very *last* word. Put together, these two words can tell you the range of words on those two pages you have open: on the pages opposite this is 'hero' to 'Highness'. Using these guide words will help you to look up words more quickly.

Anagram – unscramble these letters to make a word:

I D L E B E A R S

This one is the hardest!

This is what a typical dictionary looks like:

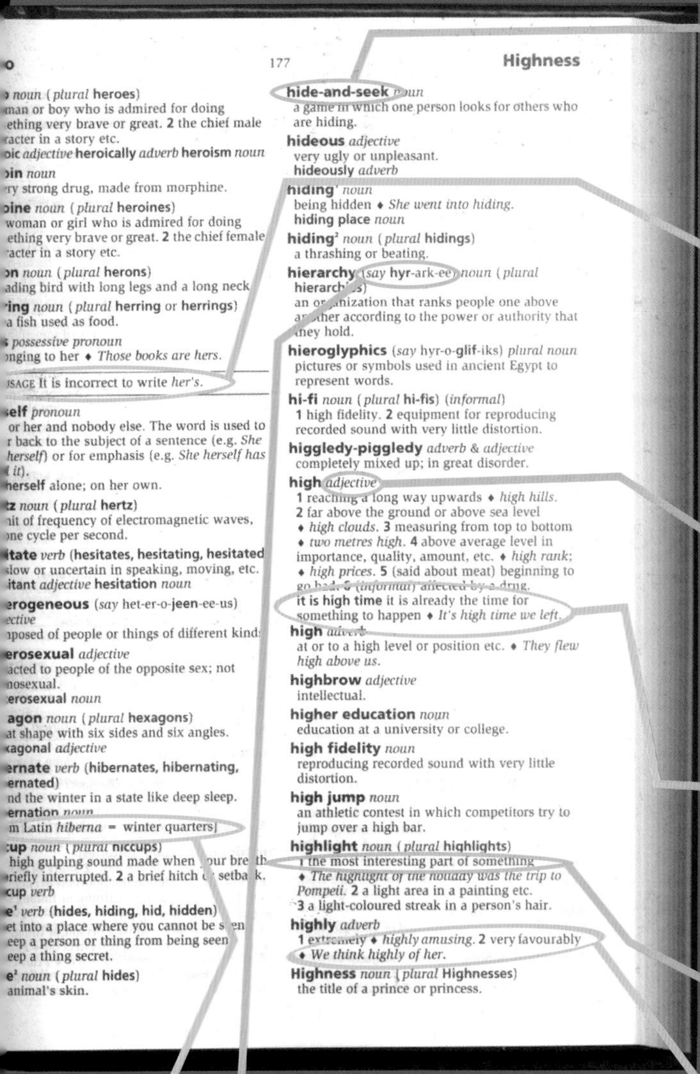

hide-and-seek Headword: this is the word that you will be looking up. It will usually be displayed in bold.

hers Usage note: these notes explain how to use tricky words correctly.

high Part of speech: this will tell you whether the headword is a noun, adjective, adverb, or preposition. Some words can be more than one.

it is high time Phrases: these are set expressions.

highlight Definition: this tells you what the headword means. Some words can mean more than one thing.

hierarchy Pronunciation help: this helps you to pronounce particularly difficult words.

highly Examples: these show how the headword is used.

hibernate Origin: this tells you the **derivation** of a word.

Dictionary column content:

heroes noun (plural heroes)
a man or boy who is admired for doing something very brave or great. **2** the chief male character in a story etc.
heroic adjective **heroically** adverb **heroism** noun

heroin noun
a very strong drug, made from morphine.

heroine noun (plural heroines)
a woman or girl who is admired for doing something very brave or great. **2** the chief female character in a story etc.

heron noun (plural herons)
a wading bird with long legs and a long neck.

herring noun (plural herring or herrings)
a sea fish used as food.

hers possessive pronoun
belonging to her ♦ Those books are hers.

USAGE It is incorrect to write her's.

herself pronoun
she or her and nobody else. The word is used to refer back to the subject of a sentence (e.g. She hurt herself) or for emphasis (e.g. She herself has done it). **by herself** alone; on her own.

hertz noun (plural hertz)
a unit of frequency of electromagnetic waves, equal to one cycle per second.

hesitate verb (hesitates, hesitating, hesitated)
to be slow or uncertain in speaking, moving, etc.
hesitant adjective **hesitation** noun

heterogeneous (say het-er-o-jeen-ee-us) adjective
composed of people or things of different kinds.

heterosexual adjective
attracted to people of the opposite sex; not homosexual.
heterosexual noun

hexagon noun (plural hexagons)
a flat shape with six sides and six angles.
hexagonal adjective

hibernate verb (hibernates, hibernating, hibernated)
to spend the winter in a state like deep sleep.
hibernation noun
[from Latin hiberna = winter quarters]

hiccup noun (plural hiccups)
a high gulping sound made when your breath is briefly interrupted. **2** a brief hitch or setback.
hiccup verb

hide¹ verb (hides, hiding, hid, hidden)
to get into a place where you cannot be seen. to keep a person or thing from being seen. to keep a thing secret.

hide² noun (plural hides)
an animal's skin.

hide-and-seek noun
a game in which one person looks for others who are hiding.

hideous adjective
very ugly or unpleasant.
hideously adverb

hiding¹ noun
being hidden ♦ She went into hiding.
hiding place noun

hiding² noun (plural hidings)
a thrashing or beating.

hierarchy (say hyr-ark-ee) noun (plural hierarchies)
an organization that ranks people one above another according to the power or authority that they hold.

hieroglyphics (say hyr-o-glif-iks) plural noun
pictures or symbols used in ancient Egypt to represent words.

hi-fi noun (plural hi-fis) (informal)
1 high fidelity. **2** equipment for reproducing recorded sound with very little distortion.

higgledy-piggledy adverb & adjective
completely mixed up; in great disorder.

high adjective
1 reaching a long way upwards ♦ high hills. **2** far above the ground or above sea level ♦ high clouds. **3** measuring from top to bottom ♦ two metres high. **4** above average level in importance, quality, amount, etc. ♦ high rank; ♦ high prices. **5** (said about meat) beginning to go bad. **6** (informal) affected by a drug.
it is high time it is already the time for something to happen ♦ It's high time we left.

high adverb
at or to a high level or position etc. ♦ They flew high above us.

highbrow adjective
intellectual.

higher education noun
education at a university or college.

high fidelity noun
reproducing recorded sound with very little distortion.

high jump noun
an athletic contest in which competitors try to jump over a high bar.

highlight noun (plural highlights)
1 the most interesting part of something ♦ The highlight of the holiday was the trip to Pompeii. **2** a light area in a painting etc. **3** a light-coloured streak in a person's hair.

highly adverb
1 extremely ♦ highly amusing. **2** very favourably ♦ We think highly of her.

Highness noun (plural Highnesses)
the title of a prince or princess.

'Proper' English

Dictionaries include slang as well as more formal English. They also include some words which some people consider to be incorrect, such as 'innit?'. Why is that?

In many countries, formal 'academies' have been set up to check the way language develops. France's *Académie Française*, for example, has tried to ban English words such as 'le weekend' and 'le self-service', insisting on French words instead. English has never been ruled in this way: it has always changed as its speakers need it to. Today's dictionaries reflect that. They describe language as it is being used. They do not dictate how it *should* be used.

Even though English is not 'governed', it is not true to say that it can be used in just *any* way. The main purpose of language is to *communicate*. If language became a free-for-all then very quickly we would begin to make no sense at all. For this reason, there are accepted rules about our vocabulary and grammar. Slang, for example, is not wrong, as long as it is used in the right circumstances.

> " *Slang is a language that rolls up its sleeves, spits on its hands and goes to work.* "
>
> Poet and author **Carl Sandberg**

What is slang?

Slang is informal language. Many slang words are in general use, but there are others which 'belong' to a particular group of people. So children and teenagers will often use words which their parents don't understand. It is a form of code, if you like. Can you think of any words which you and your friends use but which might puzzle others around you?

WHAT'S CRACKALACKIN?

?

Slang through the ages

We often think of slang as something very modern. Many people also consider it to be 'bad' English. In fact, slang has always been part of our language, and as long as it is used in the right context it is a valid means of expressing ourselves.

Can you guess in which decade of the twentieth century the following slang terms were first used?

hip

celeb

cool

awesome

Did you know?

The phrase 'luvvly jubbly', often heard today as a term of approval, was originally part of an ad slogan in the 1950s for the orange drink 'Jubbly'. Many of the informal slang terms we use today are older words or phrases which have come back into fashion.

Do you know... the following recent slang terms? They may not last very long, but they are certainly colourful.

Hey, what's crackalackin?: what's up?

sleb: celebrity

coinkydinky (pronounced co-inky-dinky): a coincidence

big up!: well done!

Language as code

There are many more examples in which language is used as a secret code. One of these is *rot13*, which was first developed on the Internet to keep messages within a group private. In this case, each letter is replaced with one thirteen letters ahead in the alphabet (the name stands for 'rotate by 13 letters'). Can you 'decode' the following words, which are written in *rot13*? Remember to replace each letter with one 13 letters ahead, starting again at the beginning of the alphabet if necessary. The letters and numbers grid will help you.

be	fur	gel	bar	envy

This might help!

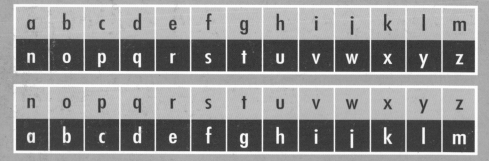

a	b	c	d	e	f	g	h	i	j	k	l	m
n	o	p	q	r	s	t	u	v	w	x	y	z

n	o	p	q	r	s	t	u	v	w	x	y	z
a	b	c	d	e	f	g	h	i	j	k	l	m

Could you develop your own secret language?

Why not start with ten words – either ones which you have invented yourself, or existing ones – and make up your very own meaning for them? Put them into alphabetical order and give each one a brief definition. If you can give an example of how they might be used, even better.

What do Becks and Posh, Shania Twain and Britney Spears all have in common? The answer is each of their names has been used as what we call 'rhyming slang' for another word. So, 'Becks and Posh' is used instead of 'nosh', 'Shania Twain' for 'pain', and 'Britney Spears' for 'beers'.

COME AND GET YOUR UNCLE FRED!

Rhyming slang first started as a secret code used by criminal gangs in the 16th, 17th and 18th centuries. By the end of the 1800s, it had become more associated with the language of London street-traders, and some of the most famous rhymes were born, such as 'apples and pears' for stairs, or 'Uncle Fred' for bread. Very often the rhyming word is left out, so 'take a butcher's' is short for 'take a butcher's hook' ('take a look') at this. Today, rhyming slang is still being used, and new rhymes are being invented. Why not have a go at making up some of your own rhymes which you can then use with your friends?

Play your own Countdown!

Why not have a go at some *Countdown* letter games yourself? You can either play against someone or simply try them on your own. Remember, the aim is to find the longest word you can out of the random selection of letters.

The answers at the foot of the page will give you some of the longer possibilities, but there will be lots more. If you're not sure of the spelling of a word, or whether it exists at all, take a look in your dictionary.

Good luck!

Round 1

E	O	T	P	T	I	R	G	N

Round 2

O	T	R	L	N	I	S	E	A

Round 3

D	F	L	S	W	I	E	N	D

Round 4

L O E D S T A R E

Round 5

P N U E T A S I M

Round 6

S G W N A V E R I

Round 7

T P S Y R E T A O

Answers

Page 11 *Blended words*

frienemy = 'friend' and 'enemy'

chofa = 'chair' and 'sofa'

globesity = 'global' and 'obesity'

Page 12 *Words from afar*

futon: Japan

silhouette: France

spaghetti: Italy (it is the plural of 'spago', meaning 'string')

kindergarten: German

ketchup: China

Page 25 *'Proper' English*

hip: 1900s

celeb: 1910s

cool: 1940s

awesome: 1960s

Page 26 *rot13*

rot13 translates these words as:

or she try one rail

Anagrams

(Congratulations, if you spotted this nine letter word!)

Glossary

abbreviation – a shortened form of a word or words, e.g. *USA* for 'United States of America'

acronym – a word or name that is made up of the initial letters of the words it is short for: e.g. *scuba* for 'self-contained underwater breathing apparatus'

anagram – a word or phrase made by rearranging the letters of another. 'Trap' is an anagram of 'part'

brand name – the name of a particular make of goods

catchword – a popular word associated with a particular fictional or real person

coin – to invent a word or phrase

compile – to put words together in a list or a collection, such as a dictionary

compound – a combination of two or more words

definition – a statement of what a word or phrase means

derivation – the origin of a word

entry – something entered in a list, diary or reference book – in this case, a dictionary

lexicographer – a person who compiles dictionaries

prefix – a word or syllable added to the beginning of a word and which changes its meaning, e.g. *un* (untidy)

slang – informal language which is used by a particular group of people

sketch – a short scene in a play or comedy

suffix – a letter or set of letters joined to the end of a word to make another one, e.g. *ful* (forgetful)